ATHEISM FOR KIDS

Jessica Thorpe

Illustrated by Teal Barnes

Winter House Books

For as long as we have been here, people have always asked questions about the world.

First published 2016 by Winter House Books

© 2016 Jessica Thorpe

Illustrations © 2016 Teal Barnes

ISBN 978-1-911560-00-5

www.winterhousebooks.com

Questions like:

Where did we come from?

Why are we here?

What happens when we die?

In the past, people told stories to help them answer difficult questions.

Why does it rain?

There is a man in the clouds who makes it rain!

Sometimes, these stories would include *gods*.

A god is a powerful being that we cannot see, who controls everything that happens in the universe.

People might say that gods created human beings, and that we should lead a good life otherwise they might be angry with us. For example:

Over time, these stories and traditions grew into *religions*.

A religion is a set of shared beliefs about the universe, which tell us why we are here and how we should live our lives.

Some of the religions that people follow today include Christianity, Buddhism and Islam.

Many people find comfort in religion, because it gives them:

Rules to live by...

Thou shalt not steal!

Answers to difficult questions...

God created us!

Shared communities and traditions...

Happy Hanukkah!

There have been many different religions throughout history, and people have believed many different things. For example:

An ancient Chinese belief was that the universe hatched from inside an egg.

The Vikings believed that the world was flat, and rested on the branches of a huge ash tree.

The Aztecs believed that the sun would only rise in the morning if it was offered enough human sacrifices.

As we learn more about the world,
we sometimes see that things people
believed in the past are not true.

For instance, we now know that the sun
does not actually need human sacrifices
to rise in the morning!

We know that it rises because
the earth rotates around the sun.

When we can explain why things happen
in the world, it becomes a lot less scary.

Lots of people today feel that religions are just based on stories from the past, and that gods do not actually exist.

People who think this are called *atheists*.

Atheism means "a lack of belief in gods".

There have been atheists for as long
as there have been people who believe
that gods exist.

Atheism is not a religion,
and atheists come from all sorts of
different backgrounds.

I am an atheist.

In fact, the only thing that atheists
have in common is that they do not
have a belief in gods!

Most atheists believe that instead of religion, we can learn about the world through *science*.

Science is a way of testing our ideas using things we find and see in the world. Something which supports our idea is called *evidence*.

Science has helped us learn a lot about the universe, and the way that things work.

Without science we would not have:

Travelled to the moon

Created vaccines
for disease

Invented the internet

Most atheists believe that we can use science to explore the big questions that we have about the universe.

For example, science has helped us understand how human beings got here.

A man called Charles Darwin suggested that animals *adapt* to their environment over time. This means that animals pass down *characteristics* to their children which will help them to survive.

For example, a bear with thick, warm fur will have a better chance at surviving in a cold environment than a bear with less fur.

The bear with thick, warm fur will survive for long enough to pass this characteristic on to its children. Over time, this means that all of the bears in that cold environment will have thick fur, as those with less fur will not have survived for long enough to have children!

This is called *evolution,* and we have found skeletons which suggest that human beings *evolved* from much smaller animals over millions and millions of years.

However, there are still questions that we do not know the answer to.

For instance, we do not know what happens to us once we die.

It is a difficult question to answer as nobody has ever returned to tell us!

Atheists do not usually believe in an afterlife.
This means they do not believe that we go to
heaven or hell after we die.

Instead, atheists usually believe that
our bodies return to the earth
and we become part of nature again.

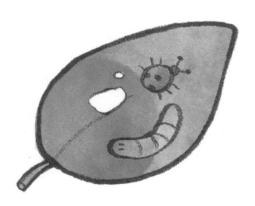

Even though it is scary to think about death,
it can be comforting to know that
we will all become part of the earth again.

If you do not believe in an afterlife,
then it is especially important to make
the most of your time on earth.

As we are only here once, we should
work hard to make life enjoyable
and happy for everyone!

Whether we are religious or not,
we can still treat people well and help
those who are less fortunate
than ourselves.

Helping other people to lead good
and happy lives can give our own
lives meaning and value.

Religious people often have rules to live by.
They learn about these rules through
religious books such as
the Bible and the Quran.

Atheists do not have a religious book
which tells them how to live.

Most atheists believe that we can make
decisions without the need for religion.

This means that human beings can know that things are right or wrong without learning it from a religious book.
For example:

We should show respect and compassion toward others.

We should not harm people or steal from them.

We should be kind toward animals.

We call these *morals* and they are a bit like rules that we can choose to live by.

Atheism is more common today
than ever before.

About 1 in 10 people in
the world are atheist.

In some countries, atheism is very common.
In the UK, about 1 in 4 people are atheist.

In other countries, however,
religion is still very important.

In Iran, about 1 in 300 people are atheist!

In countries that are very religious,
it can be dangerous to say
that you are an atheist.

This is because people can take
their religion very seriously, and might
find it offensive if you question their beliefs.

However, it is very important to respect other people's right to believe what they want, even if you do not agree with them.

Nobody should be punished for what they believe. It is okay if you are an atheist, and it is also okay if you believe in God. What is important is that we treat each other with kindness and respect.

Nobody should force you to believe
something that you do not feel is true.

You have the freedom to decide
what to believe for yourself.

This is your
right as a
human being!

What do you believe?

Do gods exist,
or were they created by
people to explain difficult things?

Did gods create human beings,
or have we evolved over time?

Is there an afterlife after we die,
or do our bodies return to nature?

Made in the USA
Monee, IL
21 October 2020